Copyright © 2015 by J. R. Wesley

All rights reserved. This book or any portion thereof may not be reproduced or used in any manner whatsoever without the express written permission of the publisher except for the use of brief quotations in a book review.

TABLE OF CONTENTS

WHY WE CARE…

SAMPLE CASE

- Aims, Objectives, & Methodologies
- Organisational Description
- Legal Considerations

HEALTH & SAFTEY MANAGEMENT REVIEW

- Description of Organisation
- Hazard Identification and Ratings
- Conclusions

RECOMMENDATIONS

- Action Planning
  - General Accident Prevention
  - Fall and Trip Accidents
  - Fire
  - Crime and Security
  - Falling Objects
  - Contractor Safety
  - Noise Control

WHY WE CARE...

According to the Health and Safety Executive (HSE), the cost of workplace injuries and disease is in excess of $15 billion dollars per year. Obviously, these figures are alarming and would suggest that Occupational Health and Safety (OHS) should be a top priority for management. Yet, a survey from 2013 revealed that many companies have no written OHS policy and nearly half have no formalized occupational health and safety program. A relatively high number of risks and hazards exist in the workplace, particularly within the retail industry. These include gas, fire and electrical dangers, personal security and violence, biological hazards, dangers from improper equipment handling, and exposure to hazardous substances.

Organisations can avoid falling into the trap of mere reactive approaches to OHS through proper education and personal responsibility. Employers have a responsibility to provide a safe and healthy workplace, properly train workers, comply with legal requirements and implement a comprehensive OHS program for their premises. Workers have a responsibility to know and follow safety requirements, work safely and report unsafe conditions and injuries immediately should an incident occur. This collaborative approach to OHS helps reduce the number of accidents in the workplace, improve staff morale, inspire confidence in management and raise competence standards which can result in significant cost savings for a business. Pre-empting negative safety issues and hazardous conditions is far better than simply responding to problems as they arise or after an accident has happened.

SAMPLE CASE

While there are many great resources out there to provide an accurate overview of OSH rules and regulations, proper application is key. For an illustrative case review, let's examine a fictitious workplace/company – Raleigh Park Shopping Centres. Let's say that you are the Building Repairs and Maintenance Manager and have been with the company since 2008. The company owns a network of indoor shopping centres and market halls, which offer a unique environment for the local independent retailer. Operator serviced retail spaces in these indoor markets, shopping halls and shopping centres provide local businesses with prime retail space with minimal levels of investment and comprehensive business support. Currently there is a network of 50 centres throughout the United Kingdom which provide trading space for over 1800 independent retailers.

Premises are normally located on high streets or attached to main shopping centres. Throughout the premises, demountable partition panels are used to sub-divide and create smaller retail units which can be leased to individual traders. Units range from 100 sq. ft. to larger units of around 400 sq. ft. or more. Each trader signs a license and is a fully independent business within the premises.

Each site is provided with a premises manager who collects weekly rent payments. In addition, cleaning staff are offered at each site to maintain the communal aisles/toilets, overall security and fire alarm systems to the premises.

The premises generally operate 6 days per week from 9am – 5pm. Site management has a degree of "duty of care" for lease holders. There is a central office that is staffed to manage human resources, accounts payable, and other business functions. There are also seven mobile handymen across the UK who carry out basic non-skilled maintenance duties. The OHS culture can best be described as "poor" and for many reasons.

For starters, the Health and Safety policies are antiquated. Those that do exist are not adequately enforced. Maintenance and safety personnel headcount is not sufficient to cover the demand and needs of the premises which means that certain preventative measures are often overlooked or poorly carried out. Lease holders are given a brief list of safety criteria and procedures, but enforcement is lacking. Shopping centre safety is the shared and collective responsibility of the mall owner and tenants, but they often have varied approaches to training staff and dealing with H&S issues. Thus, the very nature of the shopping hall business presents unique safety challenges.

Interestingly enough, the Raleigh Park corporate philosophy and mission statement is "to provide a wide range of shopping opportunities that offer value, quality and choice to all and stimulate socio-economic activity." In marketing collateral, Raleigh Park professes that its indoor markets were specifically "developed to provide an exciting shopping environment with professionally-designed, high quality shop fit units, contemporary lighting, air conditioning, security and an onsite centre management team."

The company also touts the use of higher specification materials to meet OHS standards including individual steel roller shutters, innovative signage and the like. It states that the organisation is committed to maintaining healthy local independent retailing. This would be best achieved first and foremost, by ensuring a safe work environment; however, the corporation is heavily investing in upgrading its portfolio of centres. The over-riding business objective is more about generating profits – which can sometimes mean safety shortcuts and disastrous consequences.

You believe that the company is in desperate need of a Health and Safety (H&S) audit and overhaul. Management has limited knowledge of legal compliance and, it seems, no sincere regard for the health and safety of employees, tenants or the general public. The consequences of failing to meet OHS standards could be tragic.

This is the dilemma you face in your role. You need a solid understanding of top NEBOSH and OHS considerations. This involves examining the work environment and performing an audit of the current systems in place for managing risks and hazards. By identifying shortcomings and providing H&S recommendations to management, you can inspire action, stimulate change and help minimize harm to others. Most important you will be in the best position to truly develop a well-informed, justifiable and manageable action plan.

Aims, Objectives, & Methodologies

Let's take a closer look at the current landscape of the Raleigh Park health and safety management system, hazards and risks, legal implications, and areas for improvement. Your aim is to bring conditions up to code and institute improved H&S processes necessary in retail/commercial premises. The goal is to safeguard against injury and ensure a safe and healthy work environment for all. The methodology for developing a more complete and accurate picture of current conditions includes a thorough assessment and gap analysis of the premises. You would need to carry out first-hand observation of common practices, have dialogue with mobile maintenance and cleaning staff as well as lease holders, and consultation of appropriate NEBOSH texts and legal requirements to accomplish this.

Organisational Description

As mentioned, Raleigh Park operates in-door style markets, usually within shopping centres or located on high-streets within 'Grade-B' consumer shopping areas. The premises occupied are likely to be ex-supermarket premises. These premises/buildings are gutted to shell level and specific internal layouts are produced to provide what is ultimately an indoor market of trading units leased for a minimum of three months at a time.

New traders enter into a license agreement with many clauses advising them of their health and safety responsibilities. However, conversations with tenants reveal that Raleigh Park does not have an adequate orientation or training program in place to ensure that tenants fully understand and adhere to H&S laws and legislation. Most lease holders operate autonomously within their allotted space with little to no regard for OHS policy or even basic awareness of how to handle emergency situations or report hazardous conditions or safety issues.

Management has employed seven mobile handymen to carry out the non-technical works required within the centre. These workers each cover approximately five building areas and utilize a van and basic toolkit to complete required work around the premises. The majority of their time is spent re-configuring of trading unit partition walls to accommodate new tenants. They work under the direction of the Area Manager on site and receive no consultation with senior level management.

The indoor market format of the premises presents hazards. There are many unique challenges associated with the health and safety of such shopping centres. Injuries are often commonplace due to wet floors, oily surfaces, loose rugs and mats or uneven flooring, broken tiles, spills by customers, obstructed views, poor lighting or uncovered cables. Much of the prevention of related catastrophes and accidents begins with solid housekeeping policies. This does exist throughout the Raleigh Park locations, but typically only to a minimum standard of safety, cleanliness and sanitation. Spills are typically cleaned up quickly, markers are used to highlight wet areas, and most obstacles are removed from walkways in a timely fashion. However, without proper oversight of staff, best practices are not always employed which leaves Raleigh Park open to litigation if a physical injury or another accident should occur.

In most shopping centres employees and tenants are required to have (or know where to locate) first aid kits or bags, fire extinguishers and personnel that are trained in proper equipment usage. At Raleigh Park, tenants are given little instruction in this area. In addition, employees are not adequately trained in proper lifting techniques, educated about all hazardous materials on the premises, or shown the location of material safety data sheets and how to read them. All employees should be armed with this information. Education is also needed in proper clean up techniques and what protective equipment is required for various duties (safety vests, gloves, footwear, etc.). Only safe cleaning agents should be used. With the overarching corporate focus primarily on the bottom line of the business, certain operational processes suffer from cost cutting measures such as sub-standard cleaning supplies and bare minimum stockpiles of first aid apparatuses and safety equipment.

Another important universal responsibility of commercial shopping centres involves staff training in emergency evacuation procedures. Emergency evacuation plans must be clearly communicated and displayed in order to clearly demarcate emergency exit areas. Fire safety equipment should be tested regularly under an appropriate maintenance contract. Without a top-down enforcement from senior management there is often a passive attitude in regards to conducting due diligence in fire safety and related OHS matters.

Legal Considerations

Liability is something that the company should take very seriously. The HSE conducts three main forms of regulation - guidance (not compulsory, but aimed at helping businesses comply with the law), approved codes of practice (emphasis on best practices and ways businesses can avoid dangers due to not providing relevant provisions or maintaining safe work environments); and regulations (enforcement of legal requirements). The Health and Safety at Work Act (HASAWA) 1974, sets forth the general duties that employers have towards employees and members of the public, and that employees have to themselves and to each other 'so far as is reasonably practicable'. The Management of Health and Safety at Work Regulations 1999 (the Management Regulations), offers more explicit language of what is required of employers under the HASAWA.

Control of Substances Hazardous to Health (COSHH) laws require employers to control exposure to hazardous substances – chemicals, dusts and fumes – that may cause toxic effects, infections, cancers, allergic responses, and/or asphyxiation. COSHH regulations cover substances that are dangerous to public health, including biological agents, substances with workplace exposure limits, pesticides, medicines, cosmetics and substances produced in chemical processes. Asbestos, lead, radioactive materials and substances with explosive or flammable properties are covered by other regulations. COSHH has set forth eight steps that employers and employees should undertake. They include risk assessment; taking necessary precautions; controlling exposure to hazards; ensuring use and maintenance of control measures; monitoring exposure; carrying out appropriate health surveillance; preparing accident and emergency plans; and ensuring employees are properly informed trained and supervised.

The Provision and Use of Work Equipment Regulations 1998 (PUWER) are a set of regulations that place certain requirements on businesses who own, operate or have control over work equipment. PUWER requires that equipment provided for use at work is suitable and safe for intended use, well-maintained and regularly inspected to ensure correct installation. Operators are to have received adequate information, instruction and training accompanied by suitable health and safety measures, such as protective devices and controls. These will normally include emergency stop devices, adequate means of isolation from sources of energy, clearly visible markings and warning devices used in accordance with specific requirements.

The PUWER definition of work equipment is any machinery, appliance, apparatus, tool or installation for use at work. This includes equipment which employees provide for their own use at work. The scope and use of work equipment is extremely wide and can be interpreted as "... any activity involving work equipment and includes starting, stopping, programming, setting, transporting, repairing, modifying, maintaining, servicing and cleaning."

Raleigh Park uses work equipment daily, but has not effectively managed for risks. Maintenance work is not closely monitored. Repairs and upkeep do occur as needed. However, there seems to be a failure to inspect equipment to ensure faults are proactively detected and to mitigate risks to health and safety. Written instructions and manuals regarding equipment use (as well as clear and suitable equipment markings and warning labels) are not always readily available. This means that those who actively use or manage the use of work equipment are not always adequate trained or informed. In addition, the use of the select equipment is not always restricted to only those who have been trained and appointed to use it.

Perhaps where PUWER guidelines are most lacking is where Raleigh Park' mobile handymen are concerned. Typically, businesses ensure that vehicles are properly maintained and inspected. This includes ensuring that there are fully functioning brakes, quality tires and traction systems, suitable interior restraints for drivers and passengers, proper lighting and vision equipment, routinely tested air bags in the event of a collision or rollover, and adequate liability and collision insurance. Mobile equipment should be inspected routinely; however, Raleigh Park does not have a routine mobile maintenance plan in place for its fleet of work vans.

Other key pieces of legislation that are relevant include Work at Height Regulations 2007 which calls for safeguards against falls, which can result in personal injury. Stepladders are available on the Raleigh Park premises for use by both employees and tenants. However, the company has not taken the necessary steps to ensure that all work at height is properly planned and organized or that those involved in work at height are competent. Floor surfaces are not always properly controlled and ladders used for work at height are not properly inspected and maintained.

Vibration at Work Regulations 2005 requires that motorized hand tools and machinery used on a regular basis be assessed for risk. This often affects the length of time and frequency in which equipment can be used. It also calls for annual health surveillance checks. A major challenge for Raleigh Park is that there is very little consideration given to vibration regulations when purchasing new equipment.

Noise at Work Regulations 2005 restricts excessively noisy environments and noisy equipment. On the Raleigh Park premises, tenants often use radios and CD players too loudly within their personal business units. This disrupts the shopping experience for some patrons and also disturbs neighbouring tenants. Competing noise levels from various tenants is distracting and makes it harder to hear emergency signals, fire alarms, cries for assistance, etc. Noise assessments are not carried out. Senior management has an obligation to reduce noise exposure, provide information and training for employees and issue personal hearing protection to employees as needed.

Finally, the Control of Substances Hazardous to Health (Amendment) Regulations 2004 requires implementation processes and activities that minimise the emission, release and spread of substances hazardous to health. Businesses are required to choose the most effective and reliable control options which minimise the escape and spread of substances hazardous to health. Raleigh Park does not inform and train all employees on the hazards and risks from the substances with which they work or the use of control measures developed to minimise the risks.

As a skilled professional, you are taking all of these – and more into – consideration. This is a mere non-exhaustive list of legal requirements and indicates the importance of checks and balances in workplace safety. Employers have a responsibility to ensure the health, safety and welfare of their workforce (with a written policy if there are more than five employees) to assess risks, ensure implementation of necessary protection measures, provide relevant staff training, publicize health and safety information, and report injuries and accidents. Raleigh Park employees and tenants also have a duty to take reasonable care for their own health and safety and that of others and to cooperate on health and safety matters, including the use of protection equipment and adherence to OHS policies currently in effect on the premises. It is clear from a review of current legislature and analysis of Raleigh Park processes that there are numerous hazards and risks to health and safety that exist at Raleigh Park. Let's take a closer look at this in the next section.

HEALTH & SAFTEY MANAGEMENT REVIEW

Description of Organisation

Raleigh Park, like other companies, has the added burden of senior management changing hands many times. Just last year, the company was taken over by a French company called Groupe Geraud. Groupe Geraud arranges and operates outdoor markets in the UK and Europe. Purchasing the Raleigh Park group was their first entry into the responsibility of actual 'premises'. Needless to say, they are unfamiliar with proper OHS protocol and legal compliance. The previous company owners had a dedicated H&S department responsible for its full portfolio of premises. They managed, enforced and monitored a comprehensive OHS program. The department was disbanded in 2014 when the current owners took possession. There are now two managers responsible for building 'repairs and maintenance' for the full portfolio of buildings nationwide; you and a colleague who covers the lower half of the UK. It was assumed that just two people would be adequate coverage for all health and safety management and related issues for the business properties.

Groupe Geraud inherited the OHS policies and procedures of the former owners. Those polices have not been monitored, updated or adhered to in years. In addition, and perhaps more concerning, is that there has been an almost 100% turn over in staff across the business since the company took over. New staff members are only trained in leasing units in order to turn a profit for the business. There is no accountability for the actual complex and mandatory responsibilities involved in health and safety for a building open to the public.

The benefits of the introduction of a robust and comprehensive OHS management plan are many. Foremost, there is the potential reduction in the number of accidents. Also paramount are the legal and regulatory compliance issues – this is both warranted and required. This translates into a potential reduction in public and employee liability costs and improved health, safety and welfare arrangements for those who frequent the work environment. A solid management plan demonstrates to everyone (i.e., employees, business owners, customers, and other stakeholders) management's commitment to health and safety. In short, it's good for business.

In order to fully appreciate the scope of challenges the current lack of an adequate H&S management system presents for Raleigh Park, you decide that a gap analysis against a recognized health and safety model is in order. The HSG65 (Successful Health and Safety Management) helped to establish a baseline for areas of improvement in my current organisation. As a skilled professional, you realize that any gap analysis should be tailored to the unique needs and challenges of your company, in this case commercial shopping centres and tenant focused premises. Your gap analysis covers umbrella topics as outlined by regulatory entities including:

- Policy and Organisation
- Employee and Tenant Consultation
- Information, Instruction and Training
- Performance Monitoring and Review
- Risk Assessments
- Occupational Health and First Aid
- Work Equipment
- Fire Safety and Emergency Procedures
- Personal Protective Equipment

The info that follows can be used as a checklist to determine if Raleigh Park is compliant in key categories. Each question would be marked with a "yes", "no", or "N/A." It is also helpful to code urgency. A good coding classification is:

- *Priority 1* – Recommendations that are critical and should receive management attention or planning within 3 months. Where action cannot be commenced, an action plan must be written with clear stages and expected completion dates and times.
- *Priority 2* – Recommendations that are important and must receive management attention with a view to completion within 6 months' time.
- *Priority 3* – Recommendations that are desirable and must be completed within 12 months, but which do have the potential to cause substantial impact.

Example: Are walking surfaces free from slip and fall hazards? (You note "no" because they are not, and code this item a 1 since it is an urgent need).

H&S Policy and Management
Is there a written H&S policy statement signed by senior management?
Are managers aware that they have legal H&S responsibilities?
Is there an adequate headcount of H&S staff to cover the required scope of work and number of locations?
Are regular, documented self-inspections carried out?
Are there documented H&S trainings for all staff and tenants?
Are incident, hazardous reporting, and injury forms available? Are instructions communicated for their use or how they should be filed?
Are the proper workplace H&S policies prominently displayed in a common area on the premises?
Are building and maintenance records available in the event of inspections?
Is there an H&S committee in place for the premises?
Are routine risk assessments carried out?
Is work equipment maintained and operated properly and only by specified personnel?
Is electrical equipment tested and tagged as appropriate? Is there a log book for this process?
Have trainings been delivered in niche areas such as dealing with an armed holdup, slips and falls, and other critical areas?
Are all signs in the buildings visible and in good condition?
Are danger, out of order or do not operate tags available for broken equipment?
Are heating and cooling units regularly inspected and in working condition?

Entrances and Exits
Are entrances and exits suitable for disabled access?

Are entrances and exits clearly identified?
Do entrance and exit stairs have non-slip surfaces and adequate handrails?
Are doors (particularly automated and fire) under maintenance contracts?
Do all glass areas including windows and doors have decals or other visibility aids?
Do awnings provide adequate protection from inclement weather?
Have mats and warning signs been provided on smooth surfaces, particularly during wet weather?
Is access to warehouses, maintenance and other non-public areas adequately restricted?
Are emergency exits properly signed? Are illuminated signs functional?

Internal & External Areas
Are floor coverings in good condition with no trip hazards?
Has slip resistant testing been carried out on all smooth, hard surfaces?
Have all changes in height (steps, ramps, etc.) been highlighted?
Is lighting adequate, particularly in stairwells, seating areas, hallways, restrooms and near entrances?
Is public furniture and seating regularly inspected?
Is emergency lighting installed throughout the premises and under maintenance contract?
Are indoor/outdoor smoking regulations being followed?
Is clutter and commercial equipment kept well clear of pedestrian paths?
Are controls in place in regards to power leads being run across floor surfaces?
Do all external areas have non-slip surfaces?
Is lighting adequate, particularly near footpaths and uneven surfaces?
Is all vegetation (potted plants, foliage on grounds) pruned regularly to prevent tripping and eye injury?
Are loading areas kept clear and well-lit?
Are all combustible and hazardous materials/chemicals stored securely?

Security
Have all potential security threats been identified including bomb threats, civil disturbances, assault, burglary, etc.?
Do security cameras cover all entrances and "hot spots" on the premises?
Is security footage retained for at least 30 days?
Are Security Guards present? Do they include hazard inspections in their rounds?
Is access to roof tops, basements, and service areas restricted and secured?
Are security staff trained in conflict resolution and/or dealing with aggressive behaviour?
Are cash handling procedures communicated to all tenants and staff?
Is there a work alone policy for employee well-being and an after-hours emergency number?
Are there violence and theft prevention policies and emergency procedures in place and known to all?

Emergency Procedures
Are smoke detectors and fire alarms installed throughout the premises and under maintenance contract?
Are fire and evacuation drills conducted? Are evacuation procedures displayed?

Are fire extinguishers available throughout the premises? Do employees and tenants know where they are located?

Have responsibilities for the maintenance of fire protection equipment been established by senior management?

Are emergency procedures covered in employee and tenant induction training?

Is there an incident management procedure including first aid, reporting and investigation?

When first aid supplies are used is it recorded? Are stockpiles maintained?

Are employees and tenants knowledgeable about incident reporting procedures?

Are sprinkler systems free of storage, clutter or other activities?

Are NO SMOKING signs clearly posted as appropriate? Are cigarette disposal receptacles available in designated smoking areas?

Housekeeping

Are public restrooms inspected and cleaned hourly?

Are chemicals assessed for hazardous risk?

Are regular housekeeping/cleaning performance audits carried out?

Are sufficient waste bins provided internally and externally? Are they emptied in a timely fashion?

Has proper training been provided in the operation of compactors and other waste disposal devices?

Does housekeeping staff have access to and use appropriate protective gear (footwear, gloves)?

Are waste products such as oils appropriately disposed of?

Do tenants have appropriate cleaning equipment and know how to contact housekeeping in the event of a spill?

Are service corridors, loading docks and storage areas kept clear at all times?

Tenants

Is tenant trading activity restricted in public areas?

Is tenant business activity covered by tenant liability insurance policies? Is this required to protect shoppers?

Are tenants issued specific H&S rules and policies as a customary part of lease agreements?

Do tenants receive an H&S orientation or walk-through of the premises?

Are tenants responsible for their own fire protection equipment? If so, is this closely monitored?

Contractors/Hired Help

Have contractors who work at the premises been evaluated for safe work performance?

Do contractors provide work method statements for work they perform on the premises?

Are all contractors properly oriented to the premises? Do they follow incident reporting procedures?

Do contractors hold appropriate and current public, professional and product liability insurance as applicable?

Are tools and supplies maintained properly?

Do contractors wear personal protective gear such as safety vests and hearing protection?

Are contractor supplies, sharps, and tools stored securely?

With your review and checklist complete, you have a baseline. You now need to assemble identified gaps between best practices and Raleigh Park current H&S processes and policies and make recommendations for bridging those gaps.

Hazard Identification and Ratings

Complete elimination of risk is not expected, but employers and workers share a responsibility to mitigate risks within the work environment. This includes frequent and comprehensive risk assessment:
 (1) To identify the hazards;
 (2) To decide who might be harmed and how;
 (3) To evaluate the risks and decide on precautions;
 (4) To record and implement findings;
 (5) To review risk assessment and update if necessary.

A risk assessment is an important step in protecting others and complying with the law. There are many simple and straightforward measures Raleigh Park can employ to readily control risks. Simple examples include ensuring spillages are cleaned up promptly so people do not slip. Often times a simple, inexpensive measure can ensure people and corporate assets are protected.

As the previous gap analysis and hazardous conditions list revealed, Raleigh Park has great room for improvement in nearly every area. By beginning with a basic (yet thorough) risk examination and assessment, Raleigh Park can turn a new leaf in terms of Health and Safety.

Step 1 – Identify hazards: Conduct a walk-through of the property to flag potential risks. Ask tenants and employees about concerns. Ensure HSE compliance on key issues. Check manufacturer's instructions and data sheets for chemicals and equipment. Refer back to accident and ill-health records for reference.

Step 2 - Decide who might be harmed and how: Gain clarity about who is most vulnerable to identified risks and how best to mitigate or eliminate those risks. Identify key groups (e.g., tenants, shoppers, and children). Identify what types of injuries or health dangers might occur. Include provisions for part-time employees such as special contractors. Consider upcoming or pre-planned work projects and how they may affect others.

Step 3 - Evaluate risks and decide on precautions: Create an action plan to do everything 'reasonably practicable' as required by law. Ensure it complies with industry best practice and HSE policy. Examine what is currently being done and the organisation of work tasks. Consider the controls in place and any gaps between current practice and best practice. Aim for high standards to eliminate hazards or limit exposure. Also consider welfare facilities such as first aid stations and washing stations for removing contamination. Overlooked, low-cost precautions include things such as mirrors in dangerous blind spots. Staff should be actively involved in gap analysis procedures to ensure that any suggested remedies will actually work in everyday practice and not introduce new hazards.

Step 4 - Record findings and implement them: Risk assessment results must be put into practice to make a true difference. Enforcement should come from the top down. Revised policies and procedures must be documented and communicated to all relevant parties and stakeholders. The responsibilities of the commercial facility as well as the tenants and public should be clearly defined. H&S works best when it is owned by everyone.

Step 5 - Review the assessment and update if necessary: Because work environments evolve over time, H&S policy should as well. As new equipment is acquired, new products and substances are introduced and new H&S procedures are implemented, new hazard are often created. Periodic reviews are necessary. At the conclusion of each review and risk assessment, a date for the next review should be set.

Reviews of every aspect of the business contribute towards compliance with the requirements of health and safety legislation, best practices and standards. The hazards and risks associated with each aspect of business activity require adequate and effective control measures to reduce accidents and injuries. The company is expected to demonstrate that a competent management team is in place to oversee H&S matters. This is best established with a well written policy and H&S team or committee. Plans require clear objectives and measurement tools to evaluate how well the company is meeting its objectives and standards.

A scoring system is commonly used for measuring ratings. Consider the following:

Likelihood
1 = Unlikely
2 = Possible
3 = Occasional
4 = Frequent

5 = Regular
6 = Common

Severity
1 = No injury, loss or damage
2 = Trivial injury
3 = First Aid injury
4 = Serious injury, time off but not reportable under RIDDOR
5 = Major injury & reportable
6 = Occurrence of death

Hazard Score Rating (HSR) shown for each issue is based on the combination of Severity (of potential injury) and Likelihood that the injury will occur. Example of scoring using the scale above:

If **Likelihood** selected as "possible" (score 2)
And **Severity** selected as "First Aid injury" (score 3)
Then, 2 x 3 = **Hazard Score Rating or HSR** = 6

HSR Priority Action Indicator
GREEN = LOW (1-8)
YELLOW= MODERATE (9-15)
RED = HIGH (16-36)

The following illustrates HSR analyses and calculations:

HSR Information
No H&S orientation
Lack of knowledge for personal responsibilities to ensure a safe work environment, report H&S incidents, facility provisions for lease holders, insurance obligations or emergency procedures. In the event of either major and minor emergency or health situations, tenants and employees are unaware of best practices and proper response.
L=6   S=5   HSR= 30

Vehicles
No routine inspection of van fleet

Driver and passenger safety is at risk (collisions, rollovers, etc.) In addition, vehicle accidents could create massive losses for Raleigh Park in the form of repairs, injuries and potential loss of human life.

L=5   S=5   HSR=25

Work at height

Excessive stepladder use

Stepladders are often used by employees and tenants. As well as the risks posed by the work at height itself, there are risks associated with falling objects such as paint cans, brushes, tools, or merchandise.

L=4   S=4   HRS=16

Falling objects

Improper stacking techniques in storage areas

Materials are stacked even when not absolutely necessary, (often higher than 1.5 metres). This often involves heavy materials which create a tumbling risk.

L=4   S=4   HSR=16

Personal Protective Equipment

No standardization or enforced use

Safety footwear, protective clothing, acid-resistant gloves and goggles are not standard. Without proper enforcement, employees risk personal injury.

L=4   S=4   HSR=16

Work environment

No "work alone" policies or procedures

Mobile handymen do not have control measures such as instruction, training, supervision and proper protective equipment which presents injury risk and leaves Raleigh Park vulnerable to liability issues. The company is therefore not compliant with the HSAWA 1974 or MHASAWR 1999.

L=5   S=3   HSR=15

Hazardous substances

Improper labelling of products

Employees often use hand-labelled containers for cleaning supplies.

There is no knowledge of product hazards, required precautions, and spill procedures. Raleigh Park has not provided adequate training in workplace hazardous materials best practice.

L=5   S=3   HSR=15

Electricity
Overloaded power outlets
Electricity can escape from the circuit and cause cable heating, distortion and fires.
L=3   S=4   HSR=12

Signage
Exits signs are not illuminated
There is no emergency stand-by power for illuminated exit signage. In the event of a fire or evacuation, poor visibility may create risks to personal safety and hinder escape.
L=4   S=3   HSR=12

Fire
Lack of Drills
There is no evacuation plan for the premises. The location of fire extinguishers and escape routes is not common knowledge creating a dangerous condition on the premises in the event of a fire.
L=2   S=5   HSR=10

Security
Lack of uniform security training.
Tenants may provide personal security personnel within their own business units who are given no H&S orientation and have little communication with senior management. Procedures for handling incidents of harassment, theft (or accusations), and use of force vary among shop owners. There is no consistent incident reporting to central management.
L=5   S=2   HSR=10

Information
No H&S orientation
Lack of knowledge for personal responsibilities to ensure a safe work environment, report H&S incidents, facility provisions for lease holders, insurance obligations or emergency procedures. In the event of either major and minor emergency or health situations, tenants and employees are unaware of best practices and proper response.
L=6   S=5   HSR=30

Vehicles
No routine inspection of van fleet

Driver and passenger safety is at risk (collisions, rollovers, etc.) In addition, vehicle accidents could create massive losses for Raleigh Park in the form of repairs, injuries and potential loss of human life.
L=5   S=5   HSR=25

Work at height
Excessive stepladder use
Stepladders are often used by employees and tenants. As well as the risks posed by the work at height itself, there are risks associated with falling objects such as paint cans, brushes, tools, or merchandise.
L=4   S=4   HRS=16

Falling objects
Improper stacking techniques in storage areas
Materials are stacked even when not absolutely necessary, (often higher than 1.5 metres). This often involves heavy materials which create a tumbling risk.
L=4   S=4   HSR=16

Personal Protective Equipment
No standardization or enforced use
Safety footwear, protective clothing, acid-resistant gloves and goggles are not standard. Without proper enforcement, employees risk personal injury.
L=4   S=4   HSR=16

Work environment
No "work alone" policies or procedures
Mobile handymen do not have control measures such as instruction, training, supervision and proper protective equipment which presents injury risk and leaves Raleigh Park vulnerable to liability issues. The company is therefore not compliant with the HSAWA 1974 or MHASAWR 1999.
L=5   S=3   HSR=15

Hazardous substances
Improper labelling of products
Employees often use hand-labelled containers for cleaning supplies. There is no knowledge of product hazards, required precautions, and spill procedures. Raleigh Park has not provided adequate training in workplace hazardous materials best practice.

L=5   S=3   HSR=15

Electricity
Overloaded power outlets
Electricity can escape from the circuit and cause cable heating, distortion and fires.
L=3   S=4   HSR=12

Signage
Exits signs are not illuminated
There is no emergency stand-by power for illuminated exit signage. In the event of a fire or evacuation, poor visibility may create risks to personal safety and hinder escape.
L=4   S=3   HSR=12

Fire
Lack of Drills
There is no evacuation plan for the premises. The location of fire extinguishers and escape routes is not common knowledge creating a dangerous condition on the premises in the event of a fire.
L=2   S=5   HSR=10

Security
Lack of uniform security training
Tenants may provide personal security personnel within their own business units who are given no H&S orientation and have little communication with senior management. Procedures for handling incidents of harassment, theft (or accusations), and use of force vary among shop owners. There is no consistent incident reporting to central management.
L=5   S=2   HSR=10

Sanitation/Hygiene
Public toilets not sanitized hourly
Risk of illness due to unsanitary conditions and a lack of prompt disinfection. Biological risks include contamination from blood spills or bodily waste such as solid waste, urine and/or vomit. This also has an adverse impact on the shopping experiences of patrons which is bad for business.
L=3   S=3   HSR=9

Chemical
Paint fumes

Interior painting is carried out during operational hours. Bystanders are exposed to fumes that could be harmful. There are no evacuation procedures and ventilation is inadequate. The vapours create a noxious environment that could cause, particularly to expectant mothers and children.
L=2   S=4   HSR=8

Equipment Handling
No equipment training for new staff
Power tools are sometimes allowed to "wind down" by operators. This presents a risk of injury due to moving parts. Guards are disabled at will. Employees do not employ proper techniques.
L=2   S=4   HSR=8

Ergonomics/MSIs
Maintenance tools worn out and uninspected
Tool-kits for mobile handymen are not maintained or checked routinely. Incident of a worker using a 4-pound sledgehammer with a crack that extended down the handle. This could have resulted in injury for the worker or others in the immediate area.
L=2   S=4   HSR=8

Floor Conditions
Sunken Drain Cover
There is a sunken drain cover along a high traffic pathway. It is approximately 12mm below the rest of the floor area. Anyone moving boxes held at waist height will not see the dip and could twist their ankle and fall. This could result in liability for Raleigh Park (HASAWA 1974). Costs may be incurred for the loss of staff through injury.
L=2   S=4   HSR=8

First Aid
Lack of First Aid Station in Common Area
There is no clear on-site first aid station. In the event of serious injury, employees, tenants and shoppers may go an extended period of time without aid. Re-stocking is inconsistent. Supply usage is not recorded.
L=2   S=3   HSR=6

Noise
No noise guidelines for premises

Tenants use radio and CD players too loudly. This disrupts the shopping experience for some patrons and also disturbs neighbouring tenants. Competing noise levels from various tenants is distracting and makes it harder to hear emergency signals, fire alarms, cries for help, etc.
L=3   S=2   HSR=6

Obstructions
Unsecure storage of partition walls
Idle partition walls for tenant units are placed in loosely secured areas where they tend to obstruct traffic, views and present falling risks, as well as property damage risks that could be costly to Raleigh Park.
L=3   S=2   HSR=6

Housekeeping
Reuse bins emptied infrequently
Risk of illness due to unsanitary conditions. Risk of attracting vermin to premises.
L=2   S=2   HSR=4

Conclusions

After surveying health and safety conditions at Raleigh Park and examining the risks associated with improper procedures that leave employees, tenants, and shopping mall patrons at-risk and pose liability risks for the company, it is clear that there are glaring oversights and omission in the current OHS policy. Lack of knowledge for personal responsibilities to ensure a safe work environment, report H&S incidents, tenant insurance obligations or facility emergency procedures is the chief area of danger in the work environment. In the event of both major and minor emergency and health situations, everyone would be virtually unaware of best practices and proper response.

Partition walls between units offer Raleigh Park the flexibility to lease units of different sizes. This is great for business, but the fire resistance of these walls is questionable, allowing a fire to spread and encompass other stores. In addition, there is little surveillance of tenant practices within their independent business units. Improper usage of equipment, personal heaters, and other devices present fire dangers. There are no fire drills, illuminated exit signs, evacuation procedures or basic enforcement of the H&S policies that do exist.

The situation with the mobile handymen is a major concern. Mobile handymen do not have control measures such as instruction, training, supervision and proper protective equipment. Each is given a tool-kit and a van for work use, however, maintenance is lacking. Proper liability and collision insurance is needed, as are routine vehicle inspections for the entire fleet of vans as a preventative measure against accidents.

There are numerous work at height issues including the use of stepladders by employees and tenants. This, coupled with improper stacking techniques, presents a number of risks from falling objects. In addition, there are many injury risks present due to inconsistent use protective equipment. Workers often remove safety guards from mechanical equipment and do not utilize safety footwear, protective clothing, acid-resistant gloves and goggles. Without proper enforcement of such behaviour, employees risk personal injury or creating instances of injury and dangerous conditions for others.

Sanitation and housekeeping is in place, but there is room for improvement. The nature of the shopping centre is high traffic which in turn increases the need for timely restroom cleanings and trash removal. Not only could this be costly due to disenchanted shoppers, it creates an unsanitary environment and the risk of biological hazards such as hepatitis B and other disease.

Security has room for improvement as well. The in-unit security often hired by tenants varies. Without a proper Raleigh Park H&S orientation there is no standardization in the handling of incidents of theft or harassment or incident reporting to central management. The lack of security systems and sufficient camera coverage on the premises presents a missed opportunity to hinder or deter would-be thieves.

The general public is sometimes subjected to paint fumes and high noise levels from the various businesses. This demonstrates a lack of consideration for shoppers. In general, no one follows best practices and H&S policies are not enforced. This could result in liability for Raleigh Park and prove costly in regards to the loss of staff through injury or lawsuits from tenants and visitors.

RECOMMENDATIONS

As Building Repairs and Maintenance Manager, so far as is reasonably practicable, you will need to work with management to ensure that premises and systems of work are safe and without risks to health. This includes making safe arrangements for the usage, handling, storage and transportation of equipment and substances. It is clear that adequate information is needed detailing conditions and precautions with respect to articles and substances used at work. The provision of such information, instruction, training and supervision is critical to securing the health and safety at work of all employees, tenants and shoppers.

Any premises under Raleigh Park control and operation must be in compliance with legislation. This should be appraised and updated with changes made available to all employees. There should be a Mall Safety, Health and Fire Committee instituted to help represent tenants to senior management. In addition, tenants must be made aware that it is the duty of every employee to take reasonable steps to protect their health and safety and the health and safety of other persons who may be affected by their acts or omissions at work. Tenants should fully co-operate with all health and safety arrangements in the workplace, including risk controls, safe systems and personal protective equipment.

One of the most essential components of the success of any subsequent action plans is a "top-down" enforcement of rules and regulations. Strong leadership and a clear statement regarding H&S policy adherence is an important strategic step for Raleigh Park as a corporation. This has not been demonstrated by the current managerial team overseeing the properties. There is only a very relaxed enforcement of H&S policy. Management needs to take a proactive (versus reactive) approach to health and safety issues and demonstrate strict enforcement of applicable policies. They should have hands-on involvement in gap analysis processes and H&S audits. This modelling is necessary to impact a change in behaviour in employees and tenants.

Under the HSE 1997 guidance publication 'Successful Health and Safety Management,' the case for directors/senior managers to show leadership by participating in regular health and safety tours of the workplace and appoint a 'health and safety champion' within the organisation is highlighted. In chapter 3 of HSG65, the HSE states:

> *'Visible and active support, strong leadership and commitment of senior managers and directors are fundamental to the success of health and safety management. Managers, particularly senior managers can communicate powerful signals about the importance and significance of health and safety objectives if they lead by example. Equally they can undermine the development of a positive health and safety culture through negative behaviour. Subordinates soon recognise what their superiors regard as important and act accordingly. Successful methods which signal commitment include regular health and safety tours. These are not detailed inspections but a way of demonstrating management commitment and interest and to see examples of good and bad performance. They can be planned to cover a whole site or operation progressively or to focus attention on current priorities in the overall safety effort; ...'*

Action Planning

There is overwhelming evidence that a more compliant, standardized and systematic program of H&S activities and procedures is sorely need at Raleigh Park. Once established, it must be continually updated and effectively carried out. The revamped program should relate to all aspects of occupational health and safety including:

- OHS training and education;
- provision of information to employees, contractors and sub-contractors;
- development of safe work procedures:
- emergency procedures and drills;
- provision of OHS equipment, services and facilities;
- regular workplace inspections and evaluations; and,
- reporting and recording of incidents, accidents, injuries and illnesses.

The following are hazard and risk actions you could recommend for senior management and based on evidence gathered from the previous assessments.

General Accident Prevention

Accidents can happen from cuts with a knife, injury from work equipment, carrying or moving heavy objects, chemical burns, and other dangers. General HSE protocol should not only be clarified, communicated and enforced, but monitored with regular audits.

Risk Controls (To be implemented within 3 months)

- Revised H& S policies should be distributed to all employees, contractors and tenants, with applicable policies posted in common areas;
- H&S Orientations should held for all employees, contractors and tenants, with tenants held responsible for ensuring hired help also attend;
- Spillage should be cleared promptly. Tenants should be made aware of how to reach maintenance should they require assistance or have an emergency;
- There should be clearly marked first-aid kits and/or washing stations erected and available at
- all times;
- Electrical equipment should only be used for the purpose for which it was designed and by designated personnel;
- Only a qualified electrician should be used for electrical installation work and for regular testing of portable electrical items to ensure they are in good working order;

- Equipment should never be left unattended or allowed to idle or wind down; and
- Equipment maintenance issues should be reported immediately and signposts should be used to alert others.
- Audits/inspections should be conducted every 3 months and orientations should be scheduled as needed per new tenant leases.

Fall and Trip Accidents

Common causes of office falls are uneven floor surfaces, electrical cords and wires running across walking areas or slipping on wet surfaces. Falls can also happen if a person is bending over while seated on an unstable chair or using a chair as a ladder to reach for boxes. Loose carpeting, tiles and objects temporarily stored in the general walking area or inadequate lighting are other potential risks that can result in a fall.

Risk Controls (To be implemented immediately)

- Business unit set-up, tear down and material storage should be conducted outside of operational hours when possible and done securely to protect both people and company assets;
- Premises should be kept clean, tidy, congestion-free and well lit to prevent trips, slips and falls;
- Mall furniture and stepladders should be inspected and adjusted regularly as appropriate for safe work at height conditions;
- Electrical cords and wires should be secured away from general walking areas;
- Flooring and floor coverings should be repaired or replaced, particularly on stairways and areas where the public has access;
- Spills should be cleaned up immediately to avoid slippery surfaces;
- Tenants should report to building management or the Office Manager any loose tiles, uneven carpet or broken fittings or spills on the floor; and
- Running indoors should be prohibited.
- Policy and compliance reviews should be conducted as needed or at a minimum every 6 months.

Fire

Malls, like any retailing centre, face substantial public liability exposure for fire. Crowds, obscure escape routes, inadequate protection and evacuation procedures all exasperate fire hazards. In addition, volatile plastics and chemicals used on the premises can emit killing chemical fumes and smoke.

Risk Controls (to be implemented within 3 months)

- A fire drill and evacuation plan should be created and carried out annually;

- Combustible material should be safely and securing stored away from buildings, preferably under lock and key;
- Waste bins should be emptied more frequently and lids should be kept secure. If there is no suitable external storage, store the waste in a secure internal area;
- Overloaded power strips should be eliminated and consistent monitoring in this area instituted;
- Frequent visual inspections of all portable electrical items and fixed electrical wiring should be carried out;
- Illuminated emergency exit signage should be linked to standby power and functioning properly;
- No smoking notices is be more prominently displayed;
- Designated smoking areas are to be kept free of combustible items such as paper, curtains, flammable liquids etc.;
- Ashtray contents should be emptied safely every day and not disposed of with other combustible waste.
- Clearly signed and unobstructed escape routes should be established, periodic fire drills instituted and staff should be made aware of evacuation procedures.
- Designated staff should be made responsible for customers' and visitors' safety in the event of an emergency evacuation of the premises;
- Combustible materials should not be stored in close proximity to gas and electrical heaters, light fittings or other heat generating equipment; and
- Tenants should be restricted from using portable heaters with naked flames or hot radiant surfaces and encouraged to use fan heaters and fluid-filled radiators as safer choices.
- Policy and compliance reviews should be conducted as needed or at a minimum every 6 months.

Crime and Security

Theft in shopping centres is always a concern. In addition, violence and aggression can occur which includes verbal and emotional abuse or threats as well as physical attacks on an individual or to property by another individual or group. Violent acts can range from assault – any touching of a person without their consent to any constant exposure to loud voices, arguments, accusations and threats directed at other people, or hinted at general reprisals. It should be understood that both males and females can be victims and perpetrators of workplace violence, as can minors.

Risk Controls (to be implemented within 6 months)

- Training or more information on how to recognise workplace violence, harassment and bullying, legal rights of staff, what to do in a violent incident should be provided to employees and tenants;

- Business owners hiring personal security for their "units" are responsible for ensuring that they have undergone H&S training and have a complete understanding of Raleigh Park policies;
- An Intruder Alarm system should be used to limit the time an intruder will have on the premises. It should be fitted and maintained by an installer registered with a nationally recognised installation body such as NSI (National Security Inspectorate) and SSAIB (Security Systems and Alarms Inspection Board);
- A Closed Circuit Television should be installed to deter and capture evidence of robbery. It should be fitted and maintained by an installer registered with a nationally recognised installation body such as NSI and SSAIB;
- As an improvement to work alone practices, access control locks on entrance doors should be used to prevent intimidation or robbery when reduced numbers of staff are working late; and
- Limited amounts of cash should be kept on the premises at all times.
- Audit/reviews should be conducted every 6 months.

Falling Objects

Office materials not stored properly can lead to objects falling on employees.

This can be due to the disorderly piling of materials or the over-packing of materials into confined spaces. Objects may also fall if not placed squarely on the designated storage area or stacked improperly. Excessive ladder use during operational hours poses a great risk of injury due to either dropping an item from above or disturbing neighboring objects.

Risk Controls (to be implemented immediately)

- Materials should be stacked in such a way that it minimises the chances of them falling down (e.g. place materials squarely on shelves, not allowing them to hang over the edge);
- Heavy objects should be stored on lower shelves or on the ground;
- Only those materials seldom used should be stored on high shelves;
- Major storage areas should have a safe and inspected step ladder appropriate in size for any employee to safely retrieve materials from the highest storage point; and
- Manually lifted loads should be carried out by at least two people who have proper training in lifting techniques which should be provided by management.
- Policy and compliance reviews should be conducted as needed or at a minimum every 6 months.

Contractor Safety

Mobile Handymen tool-kits should be maintained and replaced if worn out to prevent injury. In addition, vans should be inspected routinely to ensure safety.

Risk Controls (to be implemented within 3 months)
- Ensure motor vehicles are properly maintained and functioning well;
- Ensure proper liability and collision insurance;
- Ensure tool-kits are sufficient for intended work and inspected/replaced regularly; and
- Forbid the usage of mobile phones while driving, unless it is "hands free" and, even then, the driver should safely pull over to complete the call.
- Compliance reviews should be conducted every 6 months.

Noise Control

A high general noise level may interfere in work processes. Some of the effects of persistent noise are irritation, lack of concentration leading to increase in errors or carelessness, or an inability to hear emergency signals. Workplace stress is another potential consequence of noise pollution.

Risk Controls (to be implemented immediately)
- Tenants should keep noise levels at a minimum with policy enforcement to be handled by the Area Manager;
- The quietest equipment possible should be selected to stay within vibration and noise level compliances under law; and
- Loud equipment should be limited to areas where its effect is less detrimental and only used at times when it will have less effect on the others.
- Policy and compliance reviews should be conducted annually.

By following these simple protocols across all areas presented above, you will be well on your way to being a competent professional in the Health and Safety field.

For more information, consult the primary reference for developing this case study: HSE. Workplace health, safety and welfare. HSE Books, ISBN 978 0 7176 6277 7.

www.ingramcontent.com/pod-product-compliance
Lightning Source LLC
Chambersburg PA
CBHW082258220526
45469CB00009B/3060